WEIRD SNACKS

Weird Snacks

RON WIGGINS

Cover and illustrations by Pat Crowley

For my mother, Evelyn Wiggins

ACKNOWLEDGMENTS

Many thanks to the *Palm Beach Post* for permission to use material I've collected through my Weird Snacks contests during these past twenty-eight years as a features columnist. Pat Crowley illustrated the cover for the book and www.weirdsnacks.com but also declined interest in being paid unless I can rent him a B-24 and a crew to fly a mission over the Ploesti oil fields in Yugoslavia. Duncan MacDonald, Connie Bouchard, and Laura Dees provided indispensable help in getting this material off my IMac and to my editor. I am especially indebted to Cynthia MacGregor, Irma Hale and Catharine Rambeau for e-mailing so many friends who contributed to *Weird Snacks*.

SNACKS POPULI

When I was twelve, our preacher, the Reverend Bill Stonebreaker, admitted in front of God and the congregation that when he was a kid he stirred milk into powdered sugar, mixed in a spoonful of Hershey's chocolate syrup, and licked the icing off his finger while listening to *The Lone Ranger*. That's living. And that's what brought me to weird snacking.

My mother, Evelyn Wiggins, otherwise sane, pours lima beans directly from the can into a small dessert dish, stirs in a tablespoon of tartar sauce, and eats. (There will be a brief time out for a revulsion shudder.)

This is a Weird Snack. Despite the sound of it, it's amazingly tasty. Who would have thunk?

Weird Snacks and www.weirdsnacks.com celebrate human imagination where unlikely but yummy food combinations are concerned. I may not be able to define a Weird Snack in words, but if a novel food combination evokes yummy sounds from the taster, it qualifies.

Practically everybody with tongue, palate, and a particle of imagination has concocted an original and offbeat snack at one time or another. Or if not, they might admit under hypnotic regression that a crazed college roommate or demented sister was pretty clever to make crunchy peanut butter out of smooth peanut butter by simply stirring in a few Grape-Nuts, or that if you ever spread a little mustard on a piece of gingerbread, you'll never eat it any other way. Indeed, I suspect that the main reason Andrews McMeel Publishing agreed to do this book is that my editor, Patrick Dobson, wanted to see his favorite fast-food indulgence in print:

"Take a dill pickle slice out of your hamburger and wrap it around a French fry. Fantastic."

My personal favorite Weird Snack bespeaks a certain pride of authorship:

Buttery Sweet Popcorn Drizzle Bliss

One evening while microwaving popcorn, I was settling for the salty treat even as my mouth was set on something sweet. I found myself wondering, "How do you make popcorn balls?"

Visions of double boilers and candy thermometers and kitchen timers appeared before my eyes. Not in this lifetime—I don't cook. There had to be a minimalist approach to drizzling hot caramel on my popcorn. Then it came to me. In a trice I had pulled out a half stick of butter, a fist full of dark brown sugar, and a splash of vanilla extract. I combined the three ingredients in a small cereal bowl and nuked it for 90 seconds. But the result was an ugly, carbonized lump of smoking epoxy welded to the bowl. I reset the smoke alarm and threw out the experiment, bowl and all. I tried again.

This time I set the timer for 40 seconds and watched through the microwave window as the ingredients melted to a golden pool, then frothed up, my signal to turn off the microwave. The froth instantly subsided into a buttery, sugary, vanilly, semi-caramelized glaze. Then I drizzled it over the popcorn—and sampled.

My God, I have never tasted anything so heavenly in my life, and I ate until I couldn't hold any more.

Candy thermometers? We don't need no stinking candy thermometers! Could anything be better? It later occurred to me that if I put a generous handful of pecan bits into the bowl with my butter, brown sugar, and vanilla, I got a taste beyond Fiddle-Faddle. One problem on improving on the original drizzle is that the pecans make it so good that you keep swooning and falling off the couch and missing some of your movie.

Over the years, I've collected Weird Snacks from readers of my features column in the *Palm Beach Post* (www.palmbeachpost.com). I've also solicited them from the Internet, found a few in food newsgroups, and collected them from audience members after speaking engagements.

Weird Snacks Central used to rely on such archaic technologies as the Royal manual typewriter, the pencil, and the Apple IIc. The Internet, however, has ushered in a new era for the compilation of Weird Snacks. Many mouthwatering delights have come into www.weirdsnacks.com and deserve all the attention of those sent to us when we licked stamps (and by contributors who prefer to use the overland post).

Now let's get snacking: Ready. Set. Salivate!

Peeps Grotesque

Some evening when enjoying libations with friends, try the following:

Buy a box of Peeps (little marshmallow chicks) or marshmallow bunnies. Put them on paper plates (because you will never be able to clean the resulting mess off normal plates) and put them in the microwave. Marshmallows expand exponentially, and the chicks and bunnies grow and grow and grow. The more adult beverages you have consumed the funnier this seems to be.

An added bonus is that a point is reached when the marshmallows become like a crunchy toffee that is fabulous. Best if devoured when warm.

Rebecca Feinberg, www.weirdsnacks.com

Chewy Cheddar

While cooking various dishes involving cheddar cheese, I discovered the taste of overcooked cheddar. Now if I want a killer snack (probably literally, if you indulge too often), I take a nonstick frying pan (very important—you will have an absolute mess otherwise), drop in a heaping tablespoon of cheddar cheese, and cook it without stirring until the fat from the cheese has melted out and left a crisp, chewy mess of cheese. Take a nonstick spatula and lift out the well-cooked cheese and let it cool for a few minutes. You now have a crunchy, chewy, cheesy treat.

Mike McLain, Tequesta, Florida

Apple-Tuna Magic

It was not until late in life (I'm on the 16th fairway and I can see the clubhouse) that I was introduced to diced apples in tuna salad. The apples can be used instead of celery or onions or simply added for extra crunch. It is wonderful. Never make tuna without it. But that's not the Weird Snack. The Weird Snack is finding a bowl of tuna salad in the fridge and instead of doubling the calorie load by making a sandwich, peel and slice an apple and spread the tuna on sweet, crisp apple slices and eat. Leave enough to prevent ugly accusations.

Oh, joy, oh sublime streaming sweet apple essence blending with sea-salty tuna!

Myron Jablonski, Levittown, Long Island

3

Peanut Butter Sandwich Design Problem and the Apple Cure

Peanut butter sandwiches are gummy. Gummy is not a good mouth feel. You can fix the gummy problem once and for all by making a peanut butter-and-peeled apple slice sandwich. Crisp and sweet, the apple de-gums the sandwich so well that you don't even have to coat the roof of your mouth with WD-40 to prevent gagging from dreaded peanut butter build-up.

Thalia Cohen, Cherry Hill, New Jersey

Quickies

Maple syrup on grits.

Rachel Leveille

•

Soak 1 cup apples or peaches in chilled red wine for 3 or 4 hours.
Eat the fruit, drink the wine.

Paul Leveille

•

Dip almond or vanilla biscotti in red wine.

Michelle Putman, Los Angeles, California

•

It doesn't get any better than a slice of sharp cheddar
topped with a thick smear of blue cheese.

Jerry Richmond, Rome, Georgia

Pancake Abuse

My sister-in-law always asks for the mustard when we are having pancakes for breakfast. She was raised to eat mustard in place of syrup. This happened even before mustard was substituted for mayo by Weight Watchers. She attributes this trend to the thought that somewhere in her lineage there was some Indian blood, or so the story goes.

My first husband's parents were big in the Masonic Lodge, he as a Mason and she as an Eastern Star. The lodge quite often put on great roast beef dinners. They made the kind of gravy that only comes from huge mounds of beef being cooked long and slow.

After the dinners, they were apt to bring home some leftover gravy. In the morning they would serve this on top of pancakes. My son to this day talks of the mouthwatering roast beef gravy on pancakes.

We also had a neighbor that would get up in the middle of the night for a snack and was especially fond of shredded bread, salted peanuts, salt, and pepper in milk. I have not tried that one, but his mouth would water just talking about it.

Esther Clark, www.weirdsnacks.com

Eric's Grapefruit Abomination

Spoon grapefruit pulp into a bowl. Salt liberally. Add a splash of vinegar. Eat. Pucker. Eat. Pucker. Repeat until tooth enamel dissolves and you start screaming.

Eric Mabbagu, Orlando, Florida

State Fair Popcorn

Microwave a bag of popcorn. Spray heavily with butter spray. Toss with 3 tablespoons sugar and a sprinkle of salt. You get a subtle suggestion of carnival midway popcorn balls.

Rosemary Wittrock, www.weirdsnacks.com

A Note from the Author, Your Snack Czar for Life:

CINNAMON TOAST LECTURE
FOR YOUR OWN GOOD

I'm breaking a rule here by making a snack more complicated than it really has to be. In this case, the extra step is negligible. You are used to making cinnamon toast by sprinkling sugar and cinnamon on buttered toast, right? Fine. That might be good enough.

But have you ever tried broiled cinnamon toast? If you will lightly toast your bread or bagel, really slather it with butter, sugar, and cinnamon, and then pop it under a broiler so that the ingredients melt, fuse, and then caramelize, the result is a quantum leap in deliciosity. Your broiled cinnamon toast, when prepared to perfection, produces actual strings of caramel if the toast is broken and pulled apart. This operation, by the way, is recommended to hasten cooling. Otherwise you will get a roof-of-the-mouth-scalding pizza burn that will probably result in hospitalization.

"Doctor, although the entire inside of this patient's mouth is burned beyond recognition, he was making yummy sounds when we brought him in."

Weenie Hash

This one comes in handy when you don't have bread but you still want a dog. Boil your weenies and cool sufficiently to handle. Slice each weenie in half lengthwise and then slice each half in half again lengthwise (you now have 4 long strips). Cross-cut the strips so that you have little cubes of weenie. Throw into a bowl. Then head to the fridge to see what you can find. Anything you might normally put on a hot dog is fair game.

Dice pickles of any kind or cut up onions. Make cheese cubes if you have cheese. Then add mayonnaise, mustard, ketchup, or any combination of these, and stir. Eat with a spoon. Again, anything that might top a dog is worth trying. Coleslaw or sauerkraut really work well, as does chili or cold beans.

Angela Green, www.weirdsnacks.com

Mushroom Soup and Cheese on a Raft

A family favorite: cream of mushroom soup, directly out of the can, spread on lightly toasted bread and topped with a slice of cheese. Pop it under the broiler, and when cheese starts to bubble up, take it out and dig in with a fork. Do not eat as a sandwich if you do not want scalded groinal parts.

Jim Grubbs, San Jose, California

Shrieking Tooth Nerve Endings

My son, Lee, Jr., age nine, squeezes a lemon into a glass and adds a teaspoon of salt, mixes up what must be the most corrosive mixture this side of battery acid, and sips. Sparks arc between his fillings. I tried it and must admit that I liked it, but for the sake of my tooth enamel, I'll stick to sipping dill pickle brine out of the refrigerator when my wife's out of the house.

Lee Wiggins, Sr., Atlanta, Georgia

Philadelphia Fruit Thrill

Mix marshmallow creme (store-bought in a jar) and cream cheese, and dunk sliced apples in it. Actually any fruit will do, but apples are the best. Tastes like caramel apples.

Marya J. Glur, Santa Monica, California

12

Milky Way

Not the candy bar—the evaporated-milk kiddie treat that might not be too disgusting for grown-ups. Dilute canned milk with equal amount of water; add sugar and vanilla; stir and pour over crushed ice. Chug. My older cousin, Dot, used to make this for me when I could just about hook my chin over the table and beg.

Ronnie Sapp, Jacksonville, Florida

Meat Jubilee Sandwich

This works with any sliced meat or cold cuts, but it's best with turkey breast. Put your meat on the toasted bread of your choice with cling peach slices and cherry preserves. Chow down.

Arthur Juel, www.weirdsnacks.com

Pantywaist Cocoa

Full-strength hot cocoa is too rich and heavy for me. So I use a half packet of instant cocoa mix in hot water and then spoon in gangs of Coffee-mate. Now the cocoa is just to my taste. It's creamier than half-and-half, and I have a half packet left for my next cup. And if it's at bedtime, I go to sleep dreaming of the coconut oil in the creamer congealing around my heart valves.

Your Snack Czar for Life

Hot Crackers

Louisiana Hot Sauce dribbled on saltines. Variation: Mix a small water-packed can of tuna with the hot sauce and eat as a dip with saltines.

Chani Wiggins, Washington, D.C.

Top Five Weirdo Food Nominations, www.ezboard.com

1. Corn flakes stirred into Cool Whip. Honestly, what's not to like? The crunchy goodness of corn flakes with the creamlike smoothness of Cool Whip. It's a natural combo. Sort of.
2. Frosted Flakes and vanilla ice cream
3. pepperjack cheese-and-pepper jelly sandwiches
4. onions with vinegar and hoisin sause
5. sliced tomatoes with sugar

Mao Tse Byun, www.weirdsnacks.com

Cocoa Carb Overload

I use a lot of instant oatmeal mixed with cocoa at break. If I'm really feeling decadent, I stir in Cocoa Puffs or Cocoa Krispies for crunch. Suggestion: Add a little of the crunchy stuff at a time or it will dissolve into the oatmeal if it's hot.

Mark Melcon, McMurdo Station, Antarctica

Banana Pudding in a Cup

My friend Aimee and I used to make this for a late-night snack. It's quick, tasty, and low-fat. Slice bananas, then combine with vanilla wafers in a large glass.

Fill with milk. Stir vigorously and eat. Don't crumble the wafers; they'll get soggy. Yum!

Shannon Thomason, Birmingham, Alabama

Beer-Drizzled Chocolate Cake

Simply take some tasty moist chocolate cake with frosting and drizzle some quality beer on it. Dig in—mmmmmm! This was an accidental discovery, as you can imagine.

Joseph Harrigan, www.weirdsnacks.com

How to Eat Weird Like a Fisherman

Men and even women who go down to the sea (or lake, river, streams, or pond) in boats to fish are a sorry source of Weird Snacks. To invent or even discover an original and tasty food combination requires 1 percent of the brain. Unfortunately, fishermen devote that 1 percent to the fiction that they can cause fish that aren't hungry to take in their mouths a piece of plastic or rubber that doesn't look or smell remotely like anything the fish has ever eaten.

And yet fishermen do eat when they go out on the water, consuming certain delicacies in particular ways that have a collective weirdness quotient worthy of our noble snack quest. Here, then, courtesy of *Florida Sportsman* magazine, is an excerpt from a 1979 article by Vic Dunaway, on how to eat like a fisherman:

Appetizers: Potato chips, corn chips, and cheese puffs are all acceptable. To serve, place ripped-open bag on casting deck and console. Run boat briskly for five to ten minutes. This distributes the appetizers so they are within convenient reach of fishermen in various corners of the boat, who locate them easily by the crunching sounds underfoot.

Vienna Sausage: Remove lid from can and drain liquid over the side, taking care it does not come in contact with the boat hull, as it may dissolve aluminum or Gelcoat. Use brace and bit to remove first sausage from can. Discard. Serve remaining sausage to those aboard who have taken Dramamine.

Bologna Sandwiches: For each sandwich, take two slices of bread from boat's dry storage compartment. Squeeze gently for five minutes or until water no longer drips. Using spackle knife, apply evenly over bologna slices, coating both sides.

Cold fried chicken: Pick up chicken at local franchise day before trip. To serve, scrape coating from chicken and reserve for patching cracks in fiberglass. It is acceptable to eat chicken with the fingers. Fingers may be cleaned afterward with a coarse file and mineral spirits.

Sardines: Open can as far as possible (approximately $1/8$ inch) with tool or key provided. Continue opening with ice pick and pocket knife. Complete opening with screwdriver, hammer, and pliers. Wipe blood from hands before serving.

Cheese and crackers: Cut slices of processed American cheese into quarters. Insert cheese quarters between soda crackers. If cheese is not available, a third soda cracker may be substituted without adversely affecting flavor.

Potted meat: Open can with label facing you so as to avoid reading list of ingredients on the back. Dip meat from can with chips or crackers. Leftover potted meat may be stored in the refrigerator and used for buzzard repellent.

Dessert: The only acceptable angler's dessert is a chocolate bar. May be eaten with plastic spoon or soda straw, or licked directly from the wrapper.

Vic Dunaway in *Florida Sportsman*, with permission

Trust Me on This One

Into a shallow dessert bowl, heap some sweet in-their-prime strawberries. You may cut them in half if they are large, but make sure to have a few whole beauties to top this off. Then spoon on real whipped cream, the kind you beat yourself, not too sugary. Now take a good, coarse-grain pepper mill and grind just a small glitter of pepper over it all.

Eat it. It's amazing and a reminder that pepper is simply a spice, its use in no way limited to meat or entrées. A French restaurant owner/chef in Windsor, Ontario, surprised me with that twenty-five years ago, and I still eat it when I can find strawberries good enough to deserve it. I use the best black peppercorns I can find.

Catharine Rambeau, www.weirdsnacks.com

Broccoli Reprise

In high school, while hooking school one day, my girlfriend invited me over to her house and fed me *cold* leftover broccoli (had been cooked, as opposed to raw) with mayonnaise spread on it and slathered with fresh lemon juice. Still enjoy it today.

Karen Curington, Fort Lauderdale, Florida

Orange Crush and Peanuts, a Southern Favorite

Add salted peanuts to a bottle of Orange Crush. Suck and munch. Royal Crown Cola, Dr Pepper, Coke, or Pepsi can be substituted.

Your Snack Czar for Life

The Unofficial Girl Scout Potato Chip Sandwich

I learned to make the potato chip sandwich at scout camp. The essential components are chips, mayonnaise, and bread. It has to be moist. Now you can improve on the stripped-down model by going to your larder and adding mustard, ketchup, butter, sour cream, and cream cheese or cheese slices. You'll want a generous layer of potato chips, which is then smartly smashed with the top slice of bread. The chips should be pulverized for even distribution.

Potato chip sandwiches got me through college.

Angela Green, www.weirdsnacks.com

Elvis Light

Peanut butter and bacon sandwiches on toasted raisin bread—out of this world!

Patrick Crowley, Weird Snacks Cover Illustrator, West Palm Beach, Florida

(Author's note: Crowley described what essentially is a stripped-down $29.95 gourmet peanut butter sandwich that Elvis used to have shipped to him from a Colorado steak house where it was a gag item on the menu until somebody actually ordered one. The whole enchilada, so to speak, requires a loaf of sourdough bread, two pounds of bacon, a jar of Smuckers blueberry preserves, a jar of Skippy crunchy peanut butter, Mandarin orange slices, and romaine lettuce. Split the loaf lengthwise twice. Stuff the ingredients into the loaf, then try to figure out how to get any of it into your mouth.

I actually made this sandwich for a gathering of friends, using frozen sourdough bread from San Francisco. The gathering pronounced the experiment a success. The salty bacon is a wonderful counterpoint to the peanut butter and preserves.)

Olive Sandwich

Cover one slice of white bread with green salad olives (already sliced, mushed, and otherwise pulverized with pimiento). Spread the other liberally with mayonnaise, and eat, preferably with Cheer Wine, a soda pop available only in the Carolinas. It is important to use white bread for the blandness, so that the flavor of the olives comes through. I lived on olive sandwiches at lunch for an entire summer when I was eleven.

John Murphy, South Carolina

Black Forest Trick

Put ½ cup chocolate syrup and ½ cup maraschino cherry juice in the carafe of the drip coffee pot and make a pot of coffee as usual. You will have Black Forest coffee—delicious!

Dick and Barbara Melanson, Punta Gorda, Florida

Beyond Peeps

Along the same lines as nuked marshmallow Peeps (page 1) is melting a bowl of plain marshmallows in the microwave, along with a dollop of peanut butter. Keep an eye on it during cooking or you might end up with an oven full of marshmallow goo and nothing to eat! When the marshmallows have blown up to more than twice their size, take them out and mix everything together. It's basically a Fluffernutter without the bread, which would interfere with the sugar rush anyway. If you must be civilized, go ahead and spread it on a graham cracker. A Rocky Road variation of this can be made with chocolate chips and nuts instead of peanut butter.

Catharine Rambeau, www.weirdsnacks.com

Limy Frank, Peking Popcorn, Sticky Cheese

Try squeezing lime juice on your grilled hot dog. Weird, and it works. My sister puts soy sauce on popcorn. I like melted cheese on lettuce. If I'm too lazy to melt the Velveeta or whatever, I'll pinch off a leaf or two of lettuce, fold, and squiggle on some Cheez Whiz. This is best done with the refrigerator door wide open and costly cool air spilling on your feet.

Cynthia MacGregor, Lantana, Florida

Guerrilla Snacks

(FROM THE ANONYMOUS FILE)

- Peanut butter-and-banana sandwiches liberally anointed with Louisiana Hot Sauce.

- Marshmallow creme-and-mustard sandwiches.

- Saltine crackers sprinkled with lemon juice.

- Grilled cheese sandwiches dipped in corn syrup.

Alleged Eggs

My mom use to make me "eggs" for a late-night snack. Take a saltine cracker and put a large marshmallow on top, then top with a small hunk of cheddar cheese. Put them on a cookie sheet and stick under the broiler for a few minutes (until it starts to melt). Makes a wonderful study break treat!

Michele Morgan, Belle Glade, Florida

Nutty Cottage Cheese

Here's a strange combo I discovered while raiding the kitchen for any random munchables that happened to be around. I ate the last handful of unsalted peanuts, then discovered about two spoonfuls of cottage cheese and ate that while I was still tasting peanuts. The combination of flavors turned out to be quite a surprise—it was actually pretty good (or maybe I was just starving, I'm not sure).

Anyway, that led to my invention of crunchy cottage cheese. Start with 3 or 4 parts Breakstone's 4 percent small-curd cottage cheese (it's very important to use this particular cheese—most cottage cheese is inedible with a nasty aftertaste; the Breakstone is an exception). Mix with 1 or 2 parts slightly crushed (whole peanuts are too big) unsalted skinless peanuts. The best way to make it is to wait till you have used most of the cottage cheese; then you can mix it up in the cottage cheese container and you only have to clean one spoon. The peanuts can be crushed in a plastic bag by whacking them a few times with something solid.

Tom Horsley, Delray Beach, Florida

Irma's Sublime Caramel Sauce or Trip to the ER with Disfiguring Third-Degree Burns

Warning: *Do not attempt this without a fire truck parked in the driveway.*

Ah yes, sweetened condensed milk magically transformed into *dulce de leche*, the most divine caramel you ever tasted. The recipe is as follows:

Take one unopened can of sweetened condensed milk (paper removed) and put it in a pan of water so that the water covers the can. Bring to a boil, and boil for 3 hours. You will need to keep adding water periodically. *Do not ever let the water boil out!* After 3 hours you will have a wonderful caramel sauce with a consistency that is thick but pourable (something like honey). If you boil it for 4 hours the consistency will be much thicker—you will need a spoon.

Just be sure to be around for the entire time so that the water never boils away. Without the water around the can, you have a bomb on your hands.

Irma Hale, West Palm Beach, Florida

Stomach-Lining Destruction Made Tasty

Always keep cream cheese, jalapeño rings, and onions in the fridge and you will always have the makings for one of the best snack sandwiches known to man: Spread the cream cheese on rye toast, add as many jalapeño chips as you can stand, finish off with a big slice of onion, close the sandwich, and open your mouth. Sublime!

Linton Crowley, www.weirdsnacks.com

Sinus Clearing Made Simple

My friend Charlie stirs bottled horseradish into ketchup, then dips saltines in it. I scoffed. Then I tried it. Delicious!

Kathy Ptacek, Newton, New Jersey

Ice Cream Bon-bons

My own most recent, sort-of-weird snack happened at a party the other night, when we hosted the musicians from the Middlebury Wind Ensemble. I had part of a half gallon of Breyer's Dulce de Leche (caramel) ice cream and a package of instant lemon pudding. I made the lemon pudding, then, inspired by the recipe on the side of the box, added the ice cream to the cooled pudding. I tossed in some crushed pineapple and smooshed it all into ice cube trays. A couple of hours later, we popped them out of the trays and passed them at the party as finger food—sort of messy little desserts. They were a huge hit, and the recipe is in constant demand.

Improvisational variation on the caramel ice cream theme: I added some of that Dulce de Leche ice cream to cooked mashed sweet potatoes, with the remaining half of that can of crushed pineapple. It was quite well received.

Heather Masterson, Rochester, Vermont

(Ginger peachy, Heather, but did anybody eat it?)

Bettered Bagel

Lightly butter half of a bagel (any flavor). Add a coating of cream cheese, not too thick. On this place thin slices of salami (kosher is best). Cover with Swiss cheese, place in microwave for thirty to fifty seconds (or until cheese melts). Enjoy.

Phil Brenner, Lake Park, Florida

(Author's snide observation: Enjoy? The "Bettered Bagel" is about as impromptu as a Japanese tea ceremony, but worthy of mention nonetheless.)

Quickies

Maple syrup poured directly onto apple pie.

Ed Yerkes, Northville, Mississippi

•

Anybody can make and eat a peanut butter, mayonnaise, and pickle sandwich. But to actually want another one, you have to use bread-and-butter pickle chips

Jeri Matthews

•

Squeeze an orange over crushed ice, add Mountain Dew.

Lillian Heigaard

•

Pour maple syrup on cottage cheese. Tastes remarkably like butterscotch sundae with a fraction of the calories and virtually no fat.

Bill Wagar

The Derek Richards Fried Pickle

I never even heard of fried pickles until I discovered that my husband, comedian Derek Richards, is a menu item at Gary Fields's Comedy Court in Battle Creek, Michigan. While the origin of the fried pickle is disputed, author John Edge reports in *Southern Belly: The Ultimate Food Lover's Companion to the South* that the fried dill pickle was introduced at the Hollywood Cafe in Robinsonville, Mississippi, in 1969 as an act of desperation.

As the story goes, the cook ran out of catfish fillets and, figuring what the heck, battered and fried dill pickles from the barrel. The catfish batter-fried pickles went over so well that they became a featured menu item.

(Catfish batter? Sounds like work. It is. Here's how.)

Ingredients:
2 large eggs
1 cup corn meal
1/2 cup flour
2 teaspoons salt
1 teaspoon pepper

You need two bowls. Beat the eggs in one bowl and combine the corn meal, flour, salt, and pepper in the other. Thoroughly wet the whole pickles in egg mixture, then flop them around in the corn-meal mixture until coated.

In a heavy iron skillet (or deep fryer), fry the battered pickles at 375 degrees in shortening or cooking oil about three minutes on each side. Drain on paper towels.

Loretta Grantham-Richards, Globe Trotter

Loretta's Brother's Baked Chili on Potato Chips

He spreads potato chips on a cookie sheet, pours on canned chili, cheese, and onions, and bakes it.

The Author's Incredible Canned Chili Improver

The secret I am about to share will transform any chili recipe into a contender at any chili cook-off. The secret is courtesy of an unrecalled cook-off winner at a KOA Campground in Jupiter, Florida. What you do is add more chili powder than the law allows, a few teaspoons of beef bouillon, and a great big giant heap of brown sugar to counterbalance the "too much" chili powder. That's it: Add about four times the amount of powder required by any sane recipe, and then start adding dark brown sugar and taste until you love it so much you start to swoon. Don't forget the bouillon. And at the risk of getting tedious, there is no such thing as too many seared onions in your chili.

Guerrilla Snacks

(FROM THE ANONYMOUS FILE)

- Slice of bread coated with mustard and brown sugar—broil and you'll think of sugared, spiral-cut hams.

- Bread slathered with peanut butter and a layer of green salad olives.

- Cottage cheese mixed with shredded cheese, bacon bits, and salad dressing.

- Tomato soup with a generous glop of peanut butter.

Death by Cholesterol

Throw a handful of semisweet chocolate chips in the microwave, heat for 10 to 20 seconds, add a dollop of sour cream, and stir. Enjoy, but have the electric paddles ready because you can actually feel your arteries clogging.

Sharon Michaelson, www.weirdsnacks.com

All the Creatures Were Stirring

In the winter, when it is cold and you are sitting around the fire, make hot chocolate and stir it with a candy cane. Not only is it a festive and pretty way to serve the hot chocolate, it adds a really yummy flavor.

Rebecca Feinberg, www.weirdsnacks.com

Baked Bean Alchemy

Take any canned baked beans and pour off as much juice as you can. Then add two or three huge chopped seared onions and about 2 pounds of fried bacon. Add a tablespoon of apple cider vinegar and 2 tablespoons mustard. Now pour in half a bottle of smoky barbecue sauce and about a quarter box of dark brown sugar. Simmer, stirring, adding more brown sugar to taste. As with the chili secret (page 38), you want to keep adding brown sugar and tasting until you're giddy with pleasure.

Jan Terrana, Palm Beach, Florida

(Author's dubious improvement (if you dare!): To make your sweet and smoky baked beans almost inedibly hot, buy a lifetime supply of the hottest sauce known to mankind—one bottle of Endorphin Rush—and add $1/16$ teaspoon to the beans, stirring thoroughly. I'm warning you: No more than wetting the tip of the spoon in Endorphin Rush. This stuff will hurt you. They store it in Nevada, miles away from humans and groundwater. Sold through specialty stores and the Internet. Go to any search engine, type in "hot sauce," and click "Go" or "Search.")

Into the Mouths of Babes

I used to baby-sit a seven-year-old girl when I was about sixteen. Her creation falls into the category of "desperation desserts." Fill a bowl with marshmallows (or mini-marshmallows) and a scoop of butter and then microwave until melted and bubbly. Stir the gooey mixture and eat with a spoon. I must admit this is good stuff. It is important to eat the goo at just the right temperature—not so hot that it sticks to the roof of your mouth (ouch), but before it starts cooling down and turning stiff . . . very stiff.

It is also important to soak the bowl and spoon in hot soapy water immediately after finishing your snack. If you forget for a few hours you might as well throw out the bowl and spoon or find yourself a chisel.

Kathleen Slattery, Palm Beach Gardens, Florida

Roaches on a Raft

My wife, Grace, likes to slice bananas lengthwise, spread peanut butter on the flat side and then sprinkle chocolate chips on the top. My five-year-old son, Brian, says it looks like Roaches on a Raft.

Jeff Houck, West Palm Beach, Florida

Sweet and Creamy Green Slime

Scrape the goo from a very ripe avocado and mix it with canned sweetened condensed milk. Eat. This strange dessert is better if chilled, but who wants to wait?

Eric Mabbagu, Orlando, Florida

Quickies

Put a clove of garlic in oatmeal and milk.

Mom Maguire, Jupiter, Florida
(We do not challenge the contributor's claim that the Stinking
Quaker is how he takes his oats every morning, nor will we try it.)

•

Spread real mayonnaise on one slice of bread and mustard on the other.
Crush a liberal portion of regular or barbecue potato chips in between.

Cathy Yonkers

•

Spread peanut butter and sardines on rye toast.

Dorothy Bernstein, West Palm Beach, Florida

•

Eat chocolate cake with orange or tangerine slices.
Try it! You may never go back.

Rose

Onion on a Stick

I had a girlfriend once upon a time whose brother liked an onion on a stick slathered with mustard—kind of a cousin to a candy apple. For almost forty years I've thought about that kid and his mustard apples, but never actually tried it until a friend told me about weirdsnacks.com.

I couldn't find a stick, so I speared an onion with a fork and applied mustard. My wife walked in and asked me what I was doing. I told her. She said, "You're making a mess. Put the mustard in a bowl and dip it if you're going to eat it that way."

I had already taken a bite with the mustard, and it wasn't bad, but when you get down to it, since I was eating a salad on a stick, why not use salad dressing? I like croutons with my salad, so I put Hidden Valley Ranch Dressing in one bowl, crumbled croutons in the other. Then I watched a game, happily dipping my onion on a fork into ranch dressing and then into the crouton bowl to pick up just the right amount of crouton particles. Sounds like I had it down to a science, right? Wrong. The onion, while tasty, was strong, and holding it up to my face to eat it caused my eyes to water. It so happens that I'm a lap swimmer, so I went to my gym bag and got my Speedo goggles. That solved the crying problem. I was about halfway into my onion, achieving a bliss known only to Zen masters in the Seventh Absorption, when my wife walked into the living room and saw me with my half-eaten onion and my tray with salad dressing and crouton bits, wearing my swimming goggles.

"You're an idiot," she said sweetly, and left the room.

Jim Grubbs, San Jose, California

Stalking Weird Snacks on the Internet: Secret Cravings on www.pheast.com

Felicia Gonzales, writing for the Sunday, March 31, 2002, edition of pheast.com, is one of us:

"I wake up in the middle of the night and have a thundering craving for vanilla ice cream with crushed-up pretzels and corn flakes on top."

She believes people's secret food cravings tell a lot about them. "Find out what they eat with peanut butter when no one is looking and you'll get a road map to the soul."

Forget the soul, Felicia, just let us in on one of your forbidden favorites.

"Ever tried popcorn dipped in yellow mustard and maple syrup? Hey, don't knock it until you've tried it."

Knock it? We tried it. We loved it.

Guerrilla Snacks

(FROM THE ANONYMOUS FILE)

- Mayonnaise on bread sprinkled with sugar.

- Wedding cake icing—mix sugar into shortening, add a splash of vanilla, lick off the spoon.

- Leftover macaroni served in cereal bowl half filled with buttermilk.

- Peanut butter, cheese, and mustard sandwich.

- Crushed potato chips mixed with tuna salad for a sandwich with crunch.

Spread 'Em and Wrap 'Em

Pure, sublime, salty, creamy, greasy, health-destroying indulgence: I smear dill pickle chips with cream cheese and roll them in salami slices. The blend of flavors and textures thrills my taste buds and leaves an oil slick on the roof of my mouth that is easily removed by sleeping upside down on my inversion table with my mouth full of industrial degreasing solvent.

Jane Bergo, www.weirdsnacks.com

Making the Roof of Your Mouth Stink

We were out of jam, so I put some crushed garlic on the peanut butter sandwich in place of jam. It was good, but a bit strong. So now, as a change of pace, I just smear some toast with peanut butter and sprinkle on some garlic salt. It's a good taste.

Herschel Streit, Winnipeg, Canada

1040-EZ Therapy

When we were first dating, we basically had nothing in terms of material goods, so on or about April 15, we'd splurge and buy a really good bottle of Irish whiskey (Bushmill's, Jameson's, or something even more exotic) and a couple of pounds of really good chocolate (Hoffman's, Godiva, Lindt, etc.). Then we'd sit down to do our taxes. Irish whiskey on the rocks and dark chocolate is a match made in heaven, especially with a bit of whipped cream on the side. All three together really took the sting out of filling out the old 1040-EZ.

Jane and Terry Reilly, Fairbanks, Alaska

Cleopatra's Eye

Members of my Girl Scout troop used to cut a hole in the middle of a piece of bread, put it in a skillet, and break an egg in the hole. We cooked it on one side, flipped it, and cooked it on the other side. I remember we called it Cleopatra's Eye. We used to cook them on tin cans in the woods.

I don't know if the following qualifies as a Weird Snack, but my brothers used to dunk white bread in sweetened iced tea.

Kay Smith, Atlanta, Georgia

Jammin' Cherry

My favorite snack invention is a mix of very sharp aged cheddar cheese and cherry jam. Works great as a sandwich. The problem is that the only place I've found in South Florida to get really good cheddar is Costco, and the only cherry jam is at Winn Dixie. Oh well. By the way, it doesn't work with any other kind of jam—only cherry. Readers: You have been warned, don't go Smuckering around with other jams.

Phil Bate, West Palm Beach, Florida

No-fat Popcorn Revenge

One of my favorites is to turn the horrible no-fat microwave popcorn into something yummy: Mix together melted butter, honey, shredded coconut, and sliced almonds. Pour over popcorn and devour.

Dana Dunsell, West Palm Beach, Florida

Toast Stew

Some twenty-five years ago, I read a book by a Washington, D.C., journalist who spent winter weekends building a cabin in the mountains single-handed. By day's end he was whipped—and ravenous. He came up with a food creation that was quick, sustaining, and delicious.

He heated a pot of condensed vegetable beef soup, adding just a splash of water. While heating, he added great chunks of cheddar cheese and one tablespoon of Worcestershire sauce. As the cheese was melting, he made two slices of toast and then tore the toast into pieces directly into the pot. Without bothering to transfer the "toast stew" into a bowl, he simply attacked it with a spoon until sated, usually falling insensible into his cot and sleeping until dawn.

Your Snack Czar for Life is addicted to toast stew but is distressed to recall neither the inventor nor the name of his book.

Unsung Hero, Washington D.C.

Quickies

Mix crushed potato chips into vanilla or chocolate ice cream.
The salt and sweet works.

Sharon Michaelson

•

Mash a ripe banana and then add sour cream and sugar to taste.

Virginia Spears

•

Spread almond butter and guava jelly on pumpernickel toast.

Dan Peterson

•

Sprinkle sugar and cider vinegar over lettuce and dig in.

Sheila Nelson and Doris Mathews, Palm Beach Shores, Florida

Sinful Chocolate Sauce

Put a small scoop of ice cream in a bowl. Add a handful of semisweet chocolate chips and a bit of brown sugar and butter. Heat in microwave until mixture bubbles, stir, and heat again. Pour over ice cream.

Instant replay: You read that right, you're pouring ice cream over ice cream: small amount of ice cream, chocolate chips, brown sugar, and butter. Heat and stir twice, and pour over a fresh scoop of cold ice cream.

Kay Pelham, Atlanta, Georgia

Au Jus Orange Juice

When I was a bambino, maybe five to seven years old, I loved to make jelly-and-bologna sandwiches. I cut them in half and dipped them into orange juice.

Guy BenMoshe, Bastro, Texas

Popcorn Sandwich

Spread Kraft Miracle Whip on two slices of bread. Add a layer of fresh buttered popcorn in between, close the sandwich, and munch away. The "tang" is really yummy.

Shelli Drummond, Springfield, Illinois

(Author's note: Miracle Whip? Blehhhh!)

A Biblical Weird Snack

With no scriptural evidence whatsoever, southern comedian Brother Dave Gardner, who died in 1982, insisted that when Little David went to fight Goliath, his mama packed him a lunch.

Thus when David's brothers peered into the greasy brown paper bag brought from home and asked, "What did you brung us?" Little David replied, "Barbecued pig snouts and tomato and fried okra sandwiches, so's you have to lift fast and eat, lessen it fall through the crust."

Brother Dave Gardner, Atlanta, evangelist-style comedian

(1925–1982), from his sketch "How Little David Whupped Up on Goliath and the Philadelphians."

Peanut Butter and Sliced Apple Sandwich

Granted, a peanut butter-and-apple butter sandwich nowhere near qualifies as a Weird Snack, but what if you're out of apple butter and applesauce and you're absolutely freaking for apples?

When I was about fourteen I tried using peeled sliced apples in lieu of apple butter. Anyway, if you want to elevate perfection to unprecedented coefficients (ain't learnin' grand?), just add sliced apples to your p.b.-and-apple butter sandwich. Bliss to the 10th power!

Natalie Dearing, Buffalo, New York

Negative Universe Oreos

Top a Nilla wafer with a dollop of chocolate frosting (store-bought is easiest), and cap with another Nilla wafer. Might as well double-stuff it while you're at it.

Shannon Colavecchio, West Palm Beach, Florida

Peanut Butter and Lettuce Sandwich

Boring! Yes, how much duller can you get than a peanut butter-and-lettuce sandwich? That's what I thought until I came home late famished and could find nothing else in the house. Trust me, it works! The lettuce frees up the peanut butter, much the way sliced apples added to peanut butter moisten and sweeten a sandwich, reducing the need for taking a putty scraper to the roof of one's mouth.

Bonnie Gary, Strongsville, Ohio

Noodle Soup Fortifier

When my husband was in college he used to make Campbell's Chicken Noodle Soup and add a six-ounce can of tuna, drained, and a couple slices of American cheese to it. Heat it until the cheese melts and serve. Sounds disgusting, tastes good.

Jeannette Bair, West Palm Beach, Florida

Cornbread and Buttermilk

Your Snack Czar for Life submits this regional favorite in fond remembrance of the North Carolinian lady who introduced this regional snack to him. Once upon a warm afternoon, she took him to her kitchen and presented him with a big jelly-jar glass in which she had crumbled cornbread and filled with buttermilk. She then handed a spoon to the future founder of the Weird Snacks Institute of Higher Noshing. He recoiled as if handed a pit viper. While he liked cornbread well enough, he considered buttermilk an abomination and his gorge rose at the sight. When he declared that he had never eaten cornbread in buttermilk and never would, she regarded him with tender dismay and drawled:

"Well, darlin', if your mama didn't feed you cornbread and buttermilk after school every day, how did you grow up to be so big and strong?"

With thanks to Lynda McKinney, Sylva, North Carolina

Congealed Pineapple DiFrancesco

Sounds terrible, tastes incredible: Blend a can of diced pineapple with juice with 4 cups sour cream, 2 cups shredded cheddar cheese, and ½ cup sugar. Chill overnight.

Dominic DiFrancesco, www.weirdsnacks.com

(Author's stinging rebuke and clemency offer: Sorry, Mr. DiFrancesco, but your dessert, though simple, requires waiting, an obnoxious concept to the Eat Now policy of creative foraging practiced here at the institute. Because there is nothing to stop us from wolfing down your Congealed Pineapple before it can even think about congealing, we're going to let this one slide.)

Steak Sauce in Cottage Cheese

I work with a young lady who discovered this "treat" accidentally when copying her father, who swamped his steak with steak sauce. Her spillage got into her cottage cheese, and an addictive snack was born.

Terry Nickau, Stuart, Florida

Gag Me with a Gherkin

Mix chocolate syrup and peanut butter and eat as a dip with mini gherkins. The first morning I tried this I awoke with an empty pickle jar on the night stand.

Eugene Sadler, www.weirdsnacks.com

What Are you Pudding in That Rice?

Years ago, I watched an eight-year-old boy stir butter into his rice. Then he sprinkled sugar on the buttered rice. I tried not to notice. But then when he sprinkled cinnamon on the sweetened buttered rice and ate with gusto, it dawned on me what the little dickens had gone and done in broad daylight: made rice pudding and eaten dessert first, right in front of his mother.

Sean Pepper, Birmingham, Alabama

Tomato Juice and Rye

As I get older, I find it enjoyable to watch Barbara Walters on the ABC News while I snack on a small loaf of rye bread, which I dunk in a glass of tomato juice.

Warren Tabachnik, Westchester, New York

(Author's note: Warren, your snack is unusual. You, however, are weird.)

Gussied-Up Graham Crackers

Spread marshmallow creme on graham crackers and sprinkle with peanut butter chips and chocolate chips. A relatively low-cal alternative to s'mores.

Dick and Barbara Melanson, Punta Gorda, Florida

Gourmet Peanut Butter Sandwich

Make a pb&j sandwich. Beat an egg. Melt butter in a skillet. Dip both sides of your sandwich in the beaten egg and brown on both sides in the skillet. You won't believe the difference! I saw this discussed on the Internet in a food chat room.

Gail Hirsch, Chicago, Illinois

Crapple

I'm cheap. I love Snapple Diet Raspberry and Diet Peach iced tea in bottles, which are expensive. I like Crystal Lite fruit-flavored teas, which are cheap. (I defy anyone to tell the difference between Snapple and Crystal Lite during a blindfold taste test.) The downside of Crystal Lite is that you have to remember to mix up a fresh pitcher after running out.

Solution: I bought Snapple on sale (two 12-packs for the price of one), happily chugged the Snapple in the course of a week or two, and saved the bottles and screw-on metal caps. Then I put aside a couple of gallon milk cartons. You see what's coming, don't you? I mixed up two gallons of Crystal Lite Raspberry and Peach at a time and poured them off into my Snapple empties.

I filled more bottles with filtered tap water and keep them in the fridge for drinking and taking my vitamins and supplements. Now I never run out of "Snapple," and every time I take a hit from the refrigerator or grab a fresh bottle to take on the fly (fits perfectly in my Prizm's cup caddy), I feel like I'm getting away with something.

Dick Meltzer, Anchorage, Alaska

Quickies

Use graham crackers for jelly sandwiches. (Caution! Because the crackers are hard, the jelly tends to squoosh out when you bite down.)

Pat O'Bryan

•

Raspberry Antifreeze—Pour a package of raspberry Kool-Aid into a pitcher of orange juice and a pint of vodka to prevent freezing.

Gus Schmidt

•

Dipping in Style—Sit in front of your favorite show with a bag of Pepperidge Farm Milano cookies and dip them in champagne.

Karin Gully

Popcorn and Ice Cream Discovery

As a kid growing up in Salem, Massachusetts, my mother, Nancy Bouchard, always got a box of popcorn and an ice cream cone at the movies. She quickly learned that it was tastier to sprinkle the popcorn over the cone and enjoy the salty and sweet tastes together with each bite. Later the snack took on new life as she would sprinkle her own freshly popped popcorn over a bowl of ice cream. Her favorite concoction: salted popcorn over coffee ice cream.

Connie Bouchard, West Palm Beach, Florida

Skillet Breakfast

You pay $7.95 for a fancy breakfast where they cook everything together when you can make something like it at home for about a dollar. Just fry up some diced potatoes, and start adding onions, peppers, and torn-up bread. Then scramble some eggs right into it. Just before it's done, add a couple of handfuls of shredded cheddar cheese. Add salt and pepper to taste, or pour on ketchup.

Pat Villenue, Baltimore, Maryland

Tangsicle

I'm a fool for Dreamsicles, the orange popsicle with the ice-milk interior. You can't always find them in the freezer aisle, but a long time ago I found you can perfectly replicate the taste by spooning vanilla ice cream and orange sherbet into a bowl and eating them together. I know it's a popular taste because every so often McDonalds sells an orange milkshake that amounts to the same thing. Now they're even making creamy-orange Lifesavers.

So the other day, I'm at the market, I have Coffee-mate in the basket, and I see Tang on the shelf. I make the connection. What if you put Tang and Coffee-mate together—and by "together," I mean what if you poured some Coffee-mate and Tang into your palm and licked it?

This isn't as crazy as it sounds.

Back in the mid-1950s I played Little League Baseball and sat happily on the bench with my pals licking Lick-Um Ade out of our palms. Never heard of it? Lick-Um Ade came in grape, strawberry, lime, and cherry and was a granular mixture of fruit flavors and sugar. You dumped the stuff into your palm (a penny for a sugar packet–size serving) and licked. The stuff was sweet but tart and would pucker you good, and turn your tongue a hideous shade of the fruit flavor.

This did a number on your teeth.

I could hardly wait to get back to the car and try my idea of making Dreamsicle Lick-Um Ade. It is delicious! I'm hooked, and believe me, the orange tongue is hard to explain.

There's more.

After getting home to the kitchen, I microwaved a cup of water, then added a spoonful of Coffee-mate and then Tang. Hot Tang, to my delight, is out of this world and even better with creamer. The whole idea was to make a cold drink by adding ice, which I did, but I liked my hot Tangsicle drink even better. Is that weird enough? Do I get a prize?

Asa Kunkle, Hattiesburg, Mississippi

Next Time You're at McDonald's

Add a little salt to the fries along with a sprinkle of sugar. You'll wonder why everyone doesn't. Some people sprinkle salt and sugar on their popcorn—same principle.

Another McDonald's indulgence: Splurge on dessert by buying the baked apple pie and a small dish of the vanilla yogurt. Dump your yogurt on your pie, and you have apple pie à la mode for half of what you'd pay at Denny's.

Len Hayes, Duluth, Minnesota

Cheesy Thrill and the Triple-Threat Peanut Nutter Sandwich

Ever drop a piece of cheese into the sugar bowl? Even better if you use Velveeta—it's softer and moister, and a lot more sugar clings to it.

Maybe other people do this, but if there's peanut butter, real butter, and apple butter in the house, I make sandwiches with all three. You can substitute applesauce, but it doesn't have the kick.

Sara Garcia, San Jose, California

Tater Cheese Dogs

This is so good that if you start from scratch, you might as well make it for the whole family and call it dinner. But if you are fortunate enough to find some leftover mashed potatoes, you're in for a quick, satisfying treat: Split a nuked hotdog, pile on mashed potatoes and a chunk of cheese, and put it in the microwave long enough to melt the cheese. Sometimes I add a blob of mustard before putting on the cheese. If you broil it, it's even better, but I'm too impatient.

Tony Joe Hatyr, Lubbock, Texas

Guerrilla Snacks

(FROM THE ANONYMOUS FILE)

PB & Vanilla Ice Cream: Open a pint of ice cream and a jar of peanut butter, pinning both between thine ample thighs. Now spoon out a small amount of peanut butter and dip directly into ice cream. (Repeat until sated or somebody in the family smacks you one up alongside the head screaming, "You unspeakable pig, there are other people in this family!" You should strive for a pensive expression, softly replying, "Well then, Miss [Mr.] Hygiene, am I to assume you don't want me back-washing the orange juice back into the carton after I've been into the liverwurst?")

Pennsylvania Dutch Treat

This is almost too unhealthy for words. Its redeeming feature is that it's awfully tasty. Back on the farm, Mom would make us toast and spread a thin film of the bacon grease she collected in a can under the sink. Sprinkle with salt and pepper, and pop it in the microwave for 7 or 8 seconds, just enough to warm it. Then ask yourself: Why would this be any worse for you than toast and butter?

Marilyn Millar, Mechanicsville, Pennsylvania

Scalded Milk Treat

Put ¼ cup milk in a cup, fill with boiling water, add sugar and vanilla. Strange taste, but satisfying late at night.

Robert Curtis, Lead, South Dakota

Post-Party Onion Dip Salvage

Let's face it, after a party you don't want to see onion dip for a while. However, on one occasion a few years back, there was nothing else in the refrigerator except potato chips. I was hungry, but not in the mood for dipping. So I crumbled a huge handful of chips into the remaining dip, stirred it up and ate it with a spoon. It was so good that I make a point of hiding the dip and setting aside chips for my lunch the next day.

Connie Foliget, Manchester, England

Strawberry Cheese Snack

I hate blue cheese. I don't care for strawberry jam. Yet combined together on bread or crackers, a miracle happens: The tart, salty sharpness of the blue cheese somehow disarms the cloying, sickly sweetness of the jam, transforming the whole into a treat of surpassing sublimity. Plus, I like it a lot.

Judith Stiles, www.weirdsnacks.com

Corn Chips and Ice Cream

The wonderful taste of sugar and salt unite in salted corn chips dipped in vanilla ice cream. It's worth springing for premium ice cream and the costliest corn chips.

Joseph Harrigan, www.weirdsnacks.com

When You Scream for Ice Cream (and Your Stomach Can't Hack Milk)

I love ice cream, but it gives me a stomachache. So what I do is keep Cool Whip in the freezer so that it scoops like ice cream. I add sprinkles and Hershey's Dark Chocolate Syrup and I get my ice cream fix without paying the consequences.

Ina Sassoon, the Bronx, New York

The Spaghetti Sauce Trick— and its Successor

This isn't so much as a weird snack as the weird evolution of the way I eat spaghetti. I had some leftover gorgonzola cheese, so I crumbled some on top of my spaghetti sauce. Outstanding! Finally there came a time that I thought I had gorgonzola and didn't, and now the spaghetti didn't look right without it. I was actually considering running to the store. I went back to the fridge to make sure, and lo, here was cottage cheese. Okay, cottage cheese only looks like gorgonzola, but I put it on anyway and loved it. Sometimes I put gorgonzola *and* cottage cheese on my spaghetti.

Levi Allen Powell, Atlanta, Georgia

Dill Pickles and Mayo

If I wake up hungry in the middle of the night, I take a dill pickle spear and dip it straight into the mayonnaise jar. And since I am philosophically opposed to double-dipping, I then turn the other end around for my second dip. By that time, my hunger is assuaged and I throw away the middle section of pickle. I have a friend who does this with mustard.

Lynn Osgood, Tupelo, Mississippi

The Alleged Diet Elvis Sandwich

Mash a banana with shelled peanuts and spread on a slice of toasted whole wheat bread. Eat until slim.

Jane Minter, Delray Beach, Florida

Quickies

Place leftover white rice in a bowl and top with two pats of butter. Drench with *real* maple syrup. Microwave until the butter melts, stir, and eat with a spoon so you get all that buttery maple "gravy."

Cathy Patterson

•

Tex-Mex Popcorn—Make popcorn as usual, then after drizzling butter on it, sprinkle thoroughly with Tabasco sauce.

Rebecca Meinhart, Fort Worth, Texas

•

Creamed Applesauce—Try pouring heavy cream into applesauce.

Joan Hooks, Tarrytown, New York

(Author's aside: I did try this, Joan, and it took me back to when my dad always took his apple pie in a cereal bowl so he could pour milk on it. Delightful.)

The Real Chocolate Chip

My mom (Pat Newcomer) loves chocolate ice cream with potato chips. She puts the chips on top of the ice cream and uses her spoon to crunch them up into small bits, mixing them into the ice cream. It tastes great because you satisfy your salty and sweet cravings at the same time.

Wendy Newcomer, Nashville, Tennessee

Twisted Nut Spread

My best friend got me hooked on dipping thin, salty pretzels in Nutella (hazelnut spread with skim milk and cocoa). Nutella is thinner than peanut butter and it doesn't break the pretzels. This is really habit-forming.

Katie Wiggins, Berkeley, California

Better than Buttermilk and Cornbread

I know a lot of people from the South spoon cornbread out of a glass of buttermilk. What's even better is breaking up thin pretzels into a cereal bowl and pouring on buttermilk. By the way, some people can't drink buttermilk without upchucking. For the buttermilk-intolerant, the cornbread snack is great with sweet milk, and if you were to add a bit of vanilla and sugar, who is to say you nay?

Tammy Thigpen, Andrews, North Carolina

Guerrilla Snacks

(FROM THE ANONYMOUS FILE)

- Crunchy pb&j: Add Fritos to a peanut butter-and-jelly sandwich.

- Karo Delight—Mix peanut butter with Karo syrup until smooth. Eat as a dip with sliced apples.

- Float marshmallows in your coffee. But if you attempt putting marshmallows in your hot tea, people from England will find you and thrash you.

- Laverne and Shirley Pepsi—Fill a glass of cracked ice halfway with cold Pepsi. Wait until the fizz subsides, then fill the rest of the way with milk. Indulge!

DISSERTATION ON EATING IN MONTGOMERY, TEXAS

Growing up the eighth out of nine kids, and sharing the household with the four boys, just getting enough food was unusual. As a teen I'd fix peanut butter, jelly, and pickle sandwiches. My brother-in-law still reminds me that I got him to try it. Bread-and-butter pickles are the best.

Mom would fix us kids a poor man's milkshake from milk, vanilla, and sugar. That's it—no ice or ice cream. My all-time favorite sandwich, though, is fried bologna and mustard! Makes my mouth water to think of it!

My little brother, Donald, was the last and biggest in the family: thirteen pounds at birth, which would explain why he was the last. (He was born at home and was weighed on a fish scale, so he may have only been around eleven pounds.) He stayed big, and eating has always been a favorite pastime. He always poured syrup on everything he ate (except burgers). He may have gotten this idea from my dad. Dad would pour a can of stewed tomatoes in a pan and then add any and all left-overs that were in the fridge. No one fought him for a share of that.

My husband may be the inventor of Mexican Shark-fin Meatloaf. He makes ordinary meatloaf with picante sauce and Doritos. When the meat shrinks during cooking, the Doritos stick out, making it look like little sharks are swimming beneath the surface.

Bea Rouse

Food Heaven?

I don't consider this a weird snack, but my friends do, but only because they haven't yet tasted this *amazingly delicious taste bud treat!* Everyone, bar none, gets disgusted at the sound of the snack, but once they taste it, they're in food heaven.

Pour chili (preferably chili with meat and beans) all over a plate of French fries. Top with a couple of hot green peppers, onions, and ketchup. Then pour a vanilla milkshake all over it. Note: a vanilla ice cream cone can be substituted for the milkshake. Try it—I can guarantee you will love it!

Jill Siegal, www.weirdsnacks.com

(No, Jill, I will await corroborating feedback, or possibly barfback, from readers more intrepid than I.)

Tennessee Egg Sandwich

The following is a sandwich recipe that has been in our family for at least eighty years!

Melt butter in a frying pan and add an egg. Break the yolk and fry until hard. Meanwhile, spread peanut butter on one slice of bread and add a very thin slice of onion. Add the egg when cooked and top with ketchup, salt and pepper to taste. Yum, yum!!!!! Let me know how you like it!

Art Di Rico, Gatlinburg, Tennessee

(We go easy on the yum-yums around here, Art, and multiple exclamation marks !!!!! give us the hives. Your sandwich, however, is gushworthy. Take a bow.)

Class Act

- french fries dipped in Wendy's Frosty
- ice cream with cereal
- cheese puffs with peanut butter
- cottage cheese with cantaloupe and sunflower seeds
- banana dipped into peanut butter and syrup mixture
- baked beans stirred into macaroni and cheese

Karen Cloud's fifth-grade class, Sumter Middle School, Sumter, Florida

Watermelon and What?

Even though I heard this secondhand years ago from a friend, Edie Boehm, the image of it remains with me and should qualify in any Weird Snacks sweepstakes. Edie was dining with friends at Kreb's, a noted restaurant in Skaneateles, New York, when an elderly gent came in and was greeted like an old friend by the staff. The lone diner was promptly given a favorite window table and brought fresh watermelon swimming in hot chicken gravy, which he consumed with gusto.

Betty Ryen Breinin, Royal Palm Beach, Florida

Ants on a Log

Several contributors submitted the well-known stratagem of conning preschoolers into eating peanut butter–stuffed celery sticks by decorating them with a line of raisins and calling it "ants on a log." Cute, but hardly Weird. To achieve Weird, we propose blending honey with the peanut butter, putting a glob of the mixture on a Ritz cracker, topping with a date or prune, and calling it Dung Beetle out to Lunch on a Raft.

Catherine Gildiner, author of _Too Close to the Falls_, Lesiston, New York

Aunty Tilly's Coffee Soup

Crumble saltine crackers into a cup of coffee and eat. Okay, so you hate the sound of it. You don't know what you're missing.

Lenor Balcar, Palm Beach Shores, Florida

Quickies

TOM BROWN'S IRISH TREAT

This is from a friend who grew up in a big Catholic family in Philadelphia. When they had leftover green peas and mashed potatoes, they put mashed potatoes and peas on a slice of bread, poured on vinegar, folded the bread over, and got a vegetarian version of shepherd pie.

Mo Halley, www.weirdsnacks.com

•

Creamy Crunchy Sandwich—I love avocado sandwiches with potato chips in the middle. Creamy, yet crunchy!

Deb Johnson, Carmichael, California

•

Vulcanized Olives—Soak green olives in jalapeño juice for a week.

Bill Branch, Austin, Texas

Flaming Moe

Don't omit Homer Simpson's famous Flaming Moe: Tequila, schnapps, creme de menthe, and the secret ingredient—Krusty's Narkotik Kough Syrup. Once the liquors are mixed, the drink is set aflame.

Teri Mesner, Homer Simpson fan

Jack's Special Coffee

Put 1 cup mountain-grown coffee beans into an argyle sock. Then pour boiling water over and through the sock. When the coffee is a rich brown color, take your foot out.

**Jack Blanchard, wiseacre country and western writer
and performer, Lake Monroe, Florida**

Guerrilla Snacks

(FROM THE ANONYMOUS FILE)

- Fluffed Fruit—Mix cream cheese with marshmallow creme. Dip fruit.

- Fold a lettuce leaf over a ball of crunchy peanut butter. Eat.

- Mix apple butter and cottage cheese. Devour.

- Chocolate-Covered Chips—Pour a melted chocolate bar over thick-cut potato chips. Freeze until hardened.

- Sweet Rice—Pour just enough maple syrup over a serving of rice to coat the rice when mixed.

Author's Palm Salad

Turn on kitchen tap, rinse hand. Leave water running. Open refrigerator, dig 3 Spanish olives out of jar, place in clean hand, adding 2 croutons and, if available, 3 red kidney beans. Squirt Hidden Valley Ranch with Bacon dressing over the lot, eat directly from hand, licking palm clean. Repeat as needed. Rinse hand, wipe on pants.

Transcendental Snacking

Here it is, 12:16 A.M., and I'm eating a bowl of porridge made from buckwheat groats, seasoned with dulse flakes—i.e., ground-up seaweed.

The reason? I couldn't sleep and felt floaty. My cozy porridge had the most down-to-earth vibrations of any food in the house. The minerals in the seaweed soothe my system so deeply, I can practically feel relaxation seep into the marrow of my bones. I write books about deeper perception, such as *Aura Reading Through All Your Senses*. So my relationship to food may not be what these days passes for normal. I've been known to taste fruit at the supermarket by feeling its aura, a consumer technique also practiced by my son, who's ten. To me, food is frequencies of energy. I choose my comfort foods based not just on the allure of the moment, but on what the food might do to balance out my aura.

For example: split pea soup with sauerkraut revs up my second chakra, the one about sex. Revving that up brings comfort, given that there are times when I've tuned out sexiness and find it immensely reassuring just to be able to remember what the urge is like.

Cashews with blueberry jelly on rice cakes: Now that combo has been known to open up my higher chakras in order to jazz up a meditation.

Rose Rosetree, www.weirdsnacks.com

(That was much more than we wanted to know, Rose, except for the one about revving up your second chakra with sauerkraut.)

Cookie Dough Pig-out

Don't let the cookie dough title mislead you. I've never tried making cookies out of this concoction. It's just something I stir together and eat out of the bowl raw.

The idea is to take a lump of soft butter, dump some sugar on it and stir. Add just a bit of Bisquik, cinnamon, and allspice. If it's too thick, add a little milk. Just stir and then veg out in front of the tube licking off finger or spoon. I guess this snack creation comes from being in the kitchen when older relatives were making cakes and cookies. They always started by creaming together butter and sugar. I could usually get a finger full at various stages along the way.

Irma Hale, West Palm Beach, Florida

(Review: Your SCFL followed the directions above and was soon blissed out on the sofa. When I had had enough, there was about a tablespoon of dough left, enough for one theoretical cookie.

What the heck. I placed the dough on a sheet of foil sprayed with cooking spray and popped it in the toaster oven at 375 degrees and watched it carefully. The dough spread like lava and then firmed up, baking and frying in its own buttery base, small bubbles forming on the edge like a pancake. Within ten minutes, the "cookie" was brown and I took it out to cool. My gosh, it was the best cookie I have ever eaten in my life! Buttery, sugary, and chewy on the edges.)

Sinless Salsa Dip

Mix some salsa with no-fat cottage cheese and eat as a dip with no-fat restaurant-style corn chips.

Sean Nestor, www.weirdsnacks.com

Rotel Dip

Brace yourself: Rotel Dip is nothing but a one-pound brick of Velveeta cheese melted and mixed with two cans of Original Rotel (spicy) canned tomatoes. That's it. I know, it sounds disgusting. But it is disgustingly addictive.

Dice the cheese into medium chunks and dump them in a microwave-safe bowl. Toss in the Original Rotel and microwave at 50 percent power for three minutes. Stir and then microwave for another three minutes. Stir. Repeat until all the Velveeta is melted. If you have an old microwave, do whatever it takes. While the dip is working, set out a humongous sack of Tostitos or Doritos. You want to eat this stuff warm or hot, so dig in the moment it emerges from the microwave. (It can be reheated if you can't eat fast enough.)

This stuff is comfort food with no equal. You can't stop. Soon you're dipping farther and deeper into the bowl, scooping up more and more dip. Then you realize that you and your friends are hunched over the dip, nearly catatonic in your obsession. It's hard for beginners to hold up their end of the conversation because everybody's eating with such gusto and speed. Some dippers slow down after fifteen minutes or so. I slow down only when it's all gone.

Kathy Hughes, Jefferson City, Missouri

(A humbled Snack Czar for Life confesses that he was innocent of Rotel tomatoes of any kind and is now addicted to Original and Extra Hot. Kathy Hughes is right—one gets momentum while dipping Tostitos in hot Rotel Dip, and in the obsession to get more, sometimes forgets to breathe. He humbly submits his own Rotel creation, next item.)

Rotel Tomato Soup

In place of water, add one can of Rotel canned tomatoes to one can of condensed tomato soup. Add a 3-inch-thick slice of Velveeta. Heat and stir until blended. It is impossible to eat this without making urgent mewling sounds that will cause people in other rooms to attend you and ask: "Are you all right?"

Faux Salted Nut Roll

My coworker, Kris Pursell, discovered that if you combine salted peanuts with candy corn, it tastes just like a Payday candy bar. I took it a step further, added chocolate chips, and made it a Baby Ruth. Very easy—very good!

Carol Hammond, www.weirdsnacks.com

(The ladies are on to something here. The similarity is uncanny. Tiny highly satisfying variation: Sit in front of the tube with a can of walnuts and a lap full of candy corn. Pop one walnut, one kernel of candy corn in your mouth at a time. This is about as good as it gets.)

Pecos Movie House Popcorn

People in these parts put dill pickle juice on their popcorn. It has become so popular that the movie houses sell both regular and pickle. The way it works at the movies is that you buy a big kosher pickle, the kind sealed in a pack. Open the pack, carefully sprinkling the juice onto your popcorn. Naturally, the good popcorn is on top, and once you've gotten towards the middle, there's still a lot of juice left in the pickle, which you have set aside. Now you squeeze the pickle, hoping that you don't squirt juice (a) in your eye (it really smarts), or (b) down the neck of the person sitting in front of you—a tragic waste of pickle juice.

Note: Movie goers are used to getting pickle juice squirted on their necks and rarely comment unless you actually try to lick it off.

Leia Holland, Pecos, Texas

Home-Built Almond Joy

When I saw your candy corn–and–peanut trick on www.weirdsnacks.com, my first thought was, "Hey, that's my discovery." Except that when I go into the fridge, I pinch some Baker's shredded coconut, put it into my palm with any kind of nuts I have handy (walnuts, almonds, cashews) and then add two or three semisweet morsels. Your mouth can hardly tell the difference from a bit of Peter Paul Almond Joy, and you don't have to eat a whole candy bar. Okay, nobody *has* to eat a whole candy bar, but you know what I mean.

Fran Gabaldan, www.weirdsnacks.com

The Jackson Pollock

Take a hamburger bun and smear on barbecue sauce, mustard, and ketchup. Spatter with your favorite dressing and a slab of cheese for that extra kick.

Mike Kett, Winchester, Massachussetts

Tortilla to Feedya

You can make a dessert, snack, or meal from a flour tortilla. Two quick examples: Wrap fruit preserves, butter, and cream cheese in a tortilla, nuke thirty seconds, and you have dessert.

Wrap shredded cheese, meat, onion, and mayonnaise in a tortilla, nuke thirty seconds, and there's dinner.

Susan, Denton, Texas

The Almost-Too-Obvious Cream Cheese and Salsa Dip

My college roommate and I were really into the late-night snack thing. One night, we were craving a savory snack. She got out a plate and spread a packet of cream cheese directly on it. Then she topped it with chunky salsa and got out the corn chips (Fritos). We ate the dip by using the chips to scrape the dip off the plate. The cream cheese-salsa combination is so tasty, especially when combined with the salty chips, that the two of us inhaled that plate.

Tracy Kittredge, Nashua, New Hampshire

World's Zingiest Cheese Sandwich

Top rye toast with sharp cheddar cheese slices. Spread orange marmalade on the cheese evenly and broil until the cheese begins to blend with the marmalade. Outstanding.

Dante Nelson, www.weirdsnacks.com

Change of Pace Grilled Ham 'n' Cheese

If putting mustard or butter or mayo on your grilled ham and cheese gets lame, try using raisin bread and a generous dab of Thousand Island dressing. You'll never go back.

Minnie Muntz, Toledo, Ohio

Walla Walla Yummy Yummy (five snacks)

- popcorn with extra butter and a little bit of lemon juice
- coconut meat dipped in hot sauce
- peanut butter-and-potato chip sandwich
- whipped cream, Lay's Potato Chips, and M&Ms in a big bowl
- graham crackers soaked in warm water, squeezed dry, with sugar and milk added

Lenna Buissink, Walla Walla, Washington

Garlicky Cold Cooked Green Beans

Toast rye bread and spread it with mayonnaise. Sprinkle the mayo heavily with garlic powder and top with cold cooked string green beans (canned or leftover). Put salami slices on that, and top with cheddar cheese. Put it under a broiler to melt the cheese. You'll love this so much, your tongue will turn backflips.

Mac Gregory, www.weirdsnacks.com

(Cheese and rice, got all muddy, Mac, this had better be good for all that trouble.)

Quickies

Topping Secret—Put popcorn on pizza.

Elaine Deering, Boca Raton, Florida

·

Bun-nana Sandwich—Make your peanut butter-and-banana sandwich by splitting your banana and placing it in a hot dog bun.

Jerry and Alison Suffield, West Palm Beach, Florida

·

Hot Peanut Butter—Make a spreadable paste with glob of peanut butter and chili sauce. Put on crackers.

Lucie Hazel, Stuart, Florida

·

Orange Plugs and Hershey's—Put cold, seedless navel orange segments in a bowl, pour on the Hershey's chocolate syrup, and dig in.

Jeff Green, Tallahassee, Florida

The Forbidden Sandwich

I'm in seventh grade and can only get away with this when my mom goes to work early and I manage to squirrel away a plain Hershey bar. First I slice Velveeta pretty thick and put it on one slice of bread. Then I put the Hershey bar on top of the Velveeta and microwave it just enough to start the chocolate melting. No more than 15 seconds, or you get a runny mess. Anyway, the chocolate goes great with the soft Velveeta, and I'm lucky to make it to school just knowing it's in my lunch box.

Connie Truluck, Clifton, Oklahoma

Chive Cheese and Sardines

When I was a kid, I used to eat sardines and chive cheese mashed together.

Cindy Mack, www.weirdsnacks.com

Desperation Ambrosia

Some years ago, when my metabolism decided I could get along just fine on three sesame seeds a day, I started looking for tasty replacements for the usual desserts. One night before bed I had a serious hunger attack and for some reason, thought of ambrosia, that lovely mishmash of cut up oranges, sliced bananas, shredded coconut, and I don't know what all.

My snacking philosophy is that if it can't be slung together in thirty-five seconds, I'll just have a spoonful of peanut butter chased by a spoonful of boysenberry preserves. But then it occurred to me: Once you bite into orange pulp, all you taste is orange juice. So I poured orange juice into a bowl of sliced bananas. Tasty. All it really needed was shredded coconut. Then I remembered that eating an ounce of coconut is roughly equivalent cholesterol-wise to spooning down a quart of blue cheese salad dressing.

The nice thing about temptation is that it usually wins. I poured a generous handful of shredded coconut on my bananas and orange juice and had a really good time. Hint: During a commercial, put the bowl of sliced bananas in the freezer.

As for the shredded coconut, unless you're under twenty-five or have the metabolism of an electric furnace, use just enough coconut to preserve the illusion that somebody went to some trouble to make you a treat.

April Sumner, Goldfield, Iowa

When You've Done Everything Else with Peanut Butter . . .

Try stirring it in your coffee. Creamy, of course, unless you want peanut dregs in the bottom of your cup. Seriously, my first cup is straight coffee. For my second, I stir in one generous tablespoon of creamy peanut butter, and my stomach actually feels like I ate something. I'm not hungry until 11:30 A.M., and by then, my peanut protein–powered gizzard can make it to lunch.

Evelyn Knight, Louisville, Kentucky

Mango Mania

I live in South Florida, where we have mango, avocado, and key lime trees. This works with avocados, but mangoes are the best: slice the fruit and put it on bread with onions and tomatoes sprinkled liberally with lime juice. My brother does the same thing but adds mustard.

Lucinda Valdez, Miami, Florida

Just Another Ranch Dressing Idea

Probably one of the more evil things you can do with your pizza is to dip it into the little tubs of garlic butter that some takeout gives you for your bread sticks. My wife, who would probably like me to see fifty, slapped my hand and shoved the ranch low-fat dressing at me. Excellent—better than the butter and easier on the arteries.

Austin Little, Davenport, Iowa

Yes, We Have No Banana Chapter

Do you have a department called Things Improved by Adding Bananas? If so, please include slicing bananas into tomato soup. It's the old sweet-tangy, counterpoint thing, like people who break salty chips into sweet ice cream. It works in this case because tomato soup is only a little bit tangy and bananas aren't all that sweet. It'll make sense when you try it.

Malcolm Racine, Carlsbad, New Mexico

Processed Cheese and Cold Cut Death Wish

I love to put a slice of American cheese on any cold cut slice, wrap it around a pickle spear, and eat it smothered in ketchup.

Mollie B., www.weirdsnacks.com

Gooey Sandwich

I grew up in Sparta, South Carolina, where folks from the country pour molasses over just about everything they eat, especially their turnip greens and collard greens. Even sandwiches are not spared.

I confess to being addicted to making a butter-and-cheddar cheese sandwich on wheat bread, drenching it with molasses, and then eating it with a knife and fork and a big glass of sweet tea. This does not seem to be a transcultural treat—my wife, who is from New York, leaves the table.

Lonnie Mack Welch, www.weirdsnacks.com

Bulk Food

When my son needed to go up a weight class in high school wrestling, he started making himself a grilled cheese, mayonnaise, and peanut butter sandwich every day after school. Then he would put it on the plate and pour on maple syrup and eat it with a knife and fork. Once, when out of curiosity, I tried to reach for a piece of this alleged sandwich, I pulled back a bloody stump of an arm. It smelled pretty good and reminded me that in some rural areas, people pour molasses over about everything.

Rhonda Flood, Palo Alto, California

Milk and Honey and Then Some

I was cruising the Internet and ran across this one, so it's not original. Mix honey into milk with vanilla extract—it's really satisfying and can tide you over until supper.

Jill Corry, Portland, Oregon

Smucked-up Preserves

I get home from school about twenty minutes after my little sister, Jennifer. I started noticing tan flecks in the cherry preserves whenever I wanted a peanut butter-and-jelly sandwich. Turns out that Jennifer learned from a friend that sour cream–and-onion potato chips dipped into cherry preserves is really good. I explained to her that out of consideration to others, you should first take the preserves out of the jar and put it into a little bowl. But she was right, it's a nice treat.

Bobby Roundtree, Shreveport, Louisiana

Buttery Mouth Treat

Hits the spot after school: Scoop a small amount of butter with a teaspoon, dip in chocolate syrup, and lick. If you do it a second time, it's not double dipping if you're the only one in the house who drinks chocolate milk.

Jason Lobdel, Smyrna, Tennessee

That's What I Like About the South

Add some chopped onions to cold leftover black-eyed peas. Mix with mayonnaise and lemon juice or dill pickle juice. It's probably great hot, but it's so good cold when I'm starving that I never bother heating it up.

Susan Smith, Fernindina Beach, Florida

Mock Angel Cake

Sop stale bread in sweetened condensed milk, then coat the bread with shredded coconut. Grill both sides in butter until the coconut is toasted a golden, crunchy brown. Your fillings will sing you to sleep.

Janice Eddy, Delray Beach, Florida

Finnish Mule (Or How to Really Hurt Yourself with Grain Alcohol)

In a punch bowl, combine a bottle of Everclear grain alcohol, 3 or 4 cups sugar, 8 cups water, and 2 ounces each of almond extract and vanilla extract. Stir. Taste. Taste some more. Pass out. This sickly sweet killer libation has a name: Lokki.

Lorrie Hostettler, West Palm Beach, Florida

Yogurt Trick

Stir pecans and honey into coffee-flavored yogurt. If you can't find coffee-flavored yogurt, simply buy vanilla, melt a teaspoon of instant coffee in a splash of hot water and blend it into the yogurt.

Porter Crow, Waco, Texas

First Boil Your Favorite Two Poking Fingers

Then simultaneously dig one finger in crunchy peanut butter and the other into a can of chocolate icing. Suck both fingers. Like Reese's Peanut Butter Cups. Double-dipping prohibited by law in most states.

Harvey Mushman, Oxnard, California

Oatmeal Oriental

You know how it says on the oatmeal box to cook with a pinch of salt? Well, believe it or not, I couldn't find the salt, so I put soy sauce on my oatmeal. I've been eating it that way ever since.

Ellen Miller Tomioka, Palm Beach Shores, Florida

A Fonder Fondue

Dip pieces of fried venison in guava jelly. Exquisite. Almost as good if you fry Spam or even pieces of bologna and dip them in guava jelly.

Betty Luckey, Lake Park, Florida

Cream Cheese and Sour Cream Trick

I saw this in a chat room or message board, so I don't claim credit. It was so simple and tasty, and since I'd never heard of it, I'm passing it on. Just blend cream cheese and sour cream with a lot of chopped onion and use it for a sandwich spread. Really tasty and satisfying.

Little Latin Lupe Lu, www.weirdsnacks.com

Half-Hearted Peanut Butter Balls

Making real peanut butter balls is easy as pie. You just put some crunchy peanut butter in a bowl and keep stirring in oatmeal, chocolate milkshake powder, and raisins until you're happy. Then you form it into balls, chill, and it's great.

However, it's a lot easier to wait until you have a half-empty peanut butter jar and just stir the same ingredients in thoroughly. Keep it in the fridge and mine it with a spoon whenever you feel like a treat. It's probably good for you but not on purpose.

Tommie Lou Walters, Pineville, Kentucky

The Snack Czar's Hideously Complex Carrot Sauce Recipe

You will need:
4 chopped carrots
1 chopped onion
1 chopped celery stalk
1 1/2 cups chicken stock
3 cups tomato juice
1 tablespoon chili powder
1 minced garlic clove
1 tablespoon coriander
1 teaspoon oregano
1 teaspoon cinnamon

Dump the lot in a pot, bring to a boil, then simmer for half hour, stirring. Puree the mixture in a blender, starting with small amount and adding as you go. Chill. Then do Ruth Wenig's thing on the next page with the alternating layers of applesauce and carrot sauce.

Quickies

Most Counterintuitive Award—Vanilla ice cream with slices of canned grapefruit. The contrast of sweet and sour is delicious.

Kathleen Hager, New York City

·

Carrot Sauce? Applesauce!—Layer applesauce and carrot sauce (page 127), and serve it in a cup.

Ruth Wenig, Queens, New York

·

Another Dubious Applesauce "Improver"—
I adore crushed-up Oreos in applesauce.

Mary Cairnes, Crossville, Tennessee

·

Red Hot Applesauce—Sprinkle cinnamon red hots into applesauce. Lends a cinnamony bite and gives you something to chew.

Lee Wiggins, Chamblee, Georgia

Currying Flavor

Sometimes when I'm hungry and too lazy to go to any trouble, I simply mix a small amount of peanut butter and curry powder together and lick it off the spoon.

Cynthia MacGregor, Repeat Contributor, Confessed Curry Freak

Morning-After Therapy

When I was young and still at home I would treat a hangover with a sovereign cure: fried bologna with steak sauce and a can of green beans with a big slice of onion.

The only way to eat potato chips is under a big dill pickle chip. I still dip my toast in orange juice, learned from Grandma, who refused to wear her teeth and used the juice to soften up her toast for easy gumming.

Carla Million, www.weirdsnacks.com

Cake Rescue

There is no such thing as a bad or ruined cake short of charring. If the dog got into it, that should be your little secret. Here's what you do: break up the cake into small bowls, pour any fruit and juice over it with milk, whipped cream or pudding. Make sure you serve yourself the end of the cake that was farthest from the dog's mouth.

Midge Nerney, Palm Beach Shores, Florida

Garlic Heresy Bar

Ever hear of garlic cheddar cheese? Well, find some. Put a slice on a square of Hershey bar and eat.

Midge Nerney, Palm Beach Shores, Florida

Navel Biscuit

When we were kids and Dad was going to be late for dinner, Mama would give us something to tide us over. If she had leftover biscuits, she would warm them up, punch a hole in the middle with her thumb, put butter in the hole and fill it with cane syrup. It was pretty good. Not as good as it would have been with maple syrup, but in the South we didn't know there was any other kind.

Nelle Ball, Singer Island, Florida

Mongrel Bread and Molasses

In Maine, a common after-school snack is bread dipped in a pan of molasses, preferably on the back stoop. We were fortunate because my parents owned a bakery. At the end of the day, Dad would combine leftover dough from three kinds of bread and bake up a fresh loaf of "mongrel bread" for dipping. Naturally, it was fresh and still warm when we got it home.

Betty Phillips, Shelby, Maine

Franks Made Complicated

Broil or pan-fry two sliced hotdogs. While they cook, mix plenty of curry powder to taste with some mayonnaise in a bowl. Cut half an avocado into small pieces and add to the bowl. Slice the white and light green parts of four scallions. Add to the bowl. When the hot dogs are cooked, cut in thin slices and add to the bowl. Mix all the ingredients together and eat quickly while the hot dogs are still warm.

(Good gravy, Ruth, where is a body supposed to even get carrot sauce? Is there even such thing? That, of course, is a rhetorical question. We looked it up on the Internet and it turns out that you have to make it, and it is horribly *complicated*! Have we told you how much we hate complicated?)

Cynthia MacGregor (Who Actually Expects Us to Cook),
www.weirdsnacks.com

Sugar-Fried Orange Peel

This seems to be a Brooklyn treat, or at least it was popular in my neighborhood and I've never heard of it anywhere else. My mother always saved orange and lemon peels and fried them with sugar. The result was a crispy, sugary, tangy citrus peel candy. So simple, quick, and satisfying.

Elmer Klein, West Palm Beach, Florida

Chinese Keep-in

Try this one and you'll get excited every time you see leftover rice in the fridge. Throw the rice in a pan with some oil, garlic salt, soy sauce, and a little onion. Stir-fry for three or four minutes and you'll swear you've died and gone to the best Chinese restaurant in heaven.

Julie Duhl, Cypress Creek, Florida

Soothing Spaghetti

Spaghetti, my favorite food, was off limits to my super-bland reflux diet until I invented a stomach-friendly recipe. For one person: stir 1 teaspoon cornstarch into a small can of tomato juice. Heat and stir constantly until the juice is thickened and bubbly. Pour over spaghetti and top with freshly grated cheddar cheese. I could slurp this down with impunity, and if it sounds a bit bland, it's heaven for the spaghetti-deprived—all the Doug and Wendy Whiners with their diverticulitis.

Jane Zurflieh, Boynton Beach, Florida

Stepped-on Cottage Cheese

You can't do much better than pouring ketchup and black pepper on a cup of low-fat cottage cheese and digging in. And could anything be finer than white herring and onion on white bread toast?

Mack Novak, West Palm Beach, Florida

Low-Rent Pizza

Back in 1984, when my twin sister and I were attending the University of Florida, we would get matzohs and spread cottage cheese on them, add a layer of ketchup, and put it in the oven to melt. Kind of like low-fat cheap pizza. Sounds gross, but try it.

Peri Stump, Jupiter Farms, Florida

Hot Stuffed Cherry Peppers

Fill whole pickled cherry peppers with cream cheese and olives or ham if handy. You'll have to cut around the base of the peppers and pull out the stem and seeds. Excellent with beer or a glass of wine when you come home from work.

Judy Geiger, Southbury, Connecticut

We've Got Your Al Dente

Did you know that Southern kids eat raw potatoes as a snack? I know, because I had these dirt-poor friends, about ten of them, who lived next door. They would peel the potatoes, slice them like apples, and keep them in the fridge. They had to be fresh or they would taste starchy. Not bad. Better when they had a little crunchy peanut butter to spread on the wedges.

Angela Green, Prolific Contributor

Chocolate Ruffles

I have a friend who keeps a can of chocolate icing in the cupboard beside a pack of Ruffles potato chips. Whenever he wants a little snack, he takes out a chip and dips it into the chocolate. He uses Ruffles, not only because they're tasty, with a nice salt-to-chip ratio, but they're sturdy enough to dig into the icing without crumbling. Anyway, I've tried it, and you get a nice sweet-salty counterpoint taste.

Yes, you can eat just one, but only if you put the clamp back on the chips before you dip. Have the lid ready to put back on the icing, do it, close the cupboard, walk away, and nobody gets hurt.

Kelly, www.weirdsnacks.com

Surf and Nuts?

One of my *favorite* party tricks (guests *love* it!): Take a block of room-temperature cream cheese, a can of drained tuna, and a packet of dry spaghetti seasoning. Stir well and refrigerate. You can mold it—I usually shape it like a fish and cover it with slivered almonds (to look like scales). Tastes like salmon spread. *Yum.*

Karen Curington, Fort Lauderdale, Florida

(Author's note: Karen Curington's second contribution is being published with misgivings. It skirts dangerously close to being a recipe, which defies the very idea of a Weird Snack as an adventure in inspired impromptu food combinations. You're on double-secret probation on this one, Missy, and at great peril of being left out of the next edition.)

Cottage Peach Snack

It was the first morning together for me and the new love of my life. We were both starving and had to have something to eat quickly. I found some fresh peaches and diced them up. I poured peach schnapps into a bowl and tossed in the peaches to soak a while. In a separate bowl I placed plenty of cottage cheese and stirred in the soaked peaches and juice.

My girlfriend still alludes to this moment as one of our most romantic.

Chris Russell, Atlanta, Georgia

Marguerite's Twofer

1. Rice Chex coated with mayonnaise and soy sauce mixed together.
2. Soft white bread soaked with Worcestershire sauce.

Marguerite Andrews, Tampa, Florida

Tangy Chips

When I was in elementary school I would bring a lemon and hot sauce to school every day. After school I would buy a bag of Doritos and a bag of saladitos. I would sprinkle lemon juice and hot sauce on the chips for my pat-on-the-back for my hard work at school.

Susan Aquino, Los Angeles, California

Puckered Strawberries

While dining with another couple in their home last year, they promised a special treat for dessert but wouldn't tell us what it was.

After watching a video, we sipped brandies as a bowl of fresh strawberries was brought out with a nearby mound of powdered sugar and a bowl filled with some kind of liquid.

Our instructions were to dip the strawberries in the "mystery sauce" and then roll them in the powdered sugar. Wow! Tart and sweet. It wasn't until we had polished off the strawberries before we were allowed to taste the fluid straight: balsamic vinegar!

Strawberries and balsamic vinegar rolled in powdered sugar is now our favorite treat while watching golf or a movie.

Tony Napolitano and Flossie McCoy, www.weirdsnacks.com

Bosco and Vernors

In Detroit, kids stir Bosco chocolate syrup into Vernors Ginger Ale. The result tastes like chocolate-covered cherries. It doesn't make sense, but it's true. I've tried it with Hershey's syrup and store-brand el-cheapo ginger ale, and gotten comparable results. Get the Bosco and Vernors if you can.

Grey Zapitus, Detroit, Michigan

142

Georgia Breakfast

Coca-Cola and a package of Nab peanut butter crackers. I've recently moved to Atlanta and have come to realize that "Nab and Coke" and hot glazed Krispy Kreme doughnuts fuel 80 percent of Atlanta until noon.

Lynda Parnell, Atlanta, Georgia

The Very Strange Ozberry Shortcake

Spoon thick and chunky salsa onto pound cake. Top with Cool Whip. Your mind will believe that it's strawberry shortcake, but it decidedly is anything but. To prepare your palate and taste buds for the shocking contradiction to expectations, close your eyes and repeat: "Toto, I don't think we're in Kansas anymore." Now eat.

The salsa tingles your throat like a good Scotch might, but then the Cool Whip soothes the sensation and you're ready for more. Afterwards you get another chuckle out of how your taste buds were fooled by the texture and the consistency into thinking you were eating strawberries.

Michael T. Hanlon, www.weirdsnacks.com

(Author's Note: Ozberry Shortcake is the reigning Weird Snack by decree of me, Ron Wiggins, Snack Czar for Life. It is delicious, but you can't stop smiling as you eat, because every new forkful has to convince your eyes anew that you are not eating strawberries, as indeed, you aren't.)

The Last Revolting Pickle and Peanut Butter Suggestion

How about peanut butter and dill pickles, onions, mayonnaise, or all of the above? Yum-yum.

Elaine Parker, www.weirdsnacks.com

(Author's note: Sometimes I include the gratuitous "yum-yums" even when I don't trust them. Any number of people have sent variations on the theme of combining mayo, peanut butter, dill pickles, and onions. I was frankly skeptical and felt obliged to give at least one of these concoctions a shot. I mixed an experimental amount of mayo, peanut butter, and chopped onion. Then I dipped it with a dill pickle slice.

Finding: I hope I never have to choose between this alleged snack and eating peas porridge in the pot, nine days old.)

To order books or contact the author visit:

www.ronsfunnybooks.com